I0475693

Writing-Publishing Survival Guide

A General Brain-dump of Successful Self-Publishing Recipes and Systems.

By Dr. Robert C. Worstell

Table of Contents

Bonus

Who Else Wants to Write Bestsellers That Become Classics?

Get No-Charge Access to Writing and Publishing Materials from Our Library Collection

Instant Access - Join Here

Click or type into your browser:

http://livesensical.com/go/writingbooks/

Why This - Why Now?

My muse made me write this.

Just for you.

You're welcome.

Disclaimer: I've been publishing for over a decade and writing for years before that. Self-publishing was started in self-defense against the constant nagging of that muse mentioned above.

Meanwhile, I've enjoyed financial freedom for several years, meaning I fired my last boss some time back. My books started paying my bills and since then have mostly improved in sales from month to month. I live within my means while I increase those means.

The point of this was to do a final "brain dump" to get this data out in a single package of data outlining the essential points of a writing system you can follow.

And it's been called "concise" and "easy to follow" by my advanced readers.

What it doesn't have is a bunch of listicals or authoritative-sounding link-bait.

The data that supports this book is in another dozen short books I've written and published on the subject. (Check the "bonus" sections from and back to get access to them.) Or you can simply look around wherever you get your ebooks, as I probably have the copies there as well.

I make my living from writing and publishing, rinse, repeat. But I don't make a living from telling people how to write and publish. Generally, I give my hard-won knowledge mostly away for free (if you now where to look - hint: that "bonus" section again...)

In this short book, you get the outline and the bare-knuckle opinion of who I think is worth a damn to learn from. Just because I've spent a lot of time and money on courses that weren't worth it, doesn't mean you should have to.

And included in here are some "wild" theories that no one else has proved, but you can be my guest. They work for me. They help me make sense of self-publishing. And I'm about to do a couple of major tests of these, but wanted to let you know in case I don't surface from those adventures...

Meanwhile, it's over to you. Have fun.

Leave a review if you like it. Buy my other books if it's worth something to you.

Cheers!

I - The Writing & Publishing Survival Guide

A Multiple Eyeballs Theorem:

0. **Publish to all possible sales points in all possible formats.** *Be everywhere to everyone with everything you can.*

1. **Books As a Container** – the content of your book is able to be in multiple digital and print formats. It's not just ebooks and its not just print.

2. **Be on Both Sides of the Garden Walls** – No one store has all the customers. Different audiences have different preferences. Diversification is the key to sales. Every best-selling author has multiple versions available everywhere they can.

- *Ebooks* (epub, mobi, PDF – Amazon, iTunes, Nook, Kobo, Lulu.com, Scribd, 24Symbols, GooglePlay, and hundreds of others, if not thousands.)

- *audio* (audiobooks, CD's – Author's Republic, ACX, CDbaby.com)

- *print* (paperback, hardback, special bindings – Lulu, CreateSpace, IngramSpark)

- *courses* (CD/DVD, online – Udemy, Skillshare, and others with marketplaces)

- *bundles* (combinations of all these, digitally or physically delivered. - BitTorrent, various Affiliate marketplaces like JVZoo)

- *video* (iAmplify, Youtube, Vimeo, Facebook, etc. Even DVDs on Amazon and CDBaby.)

3. **Be everywhere at once** – you can't get sales you don't ask for. There are a range of places who want to help you sell your books (for a small piece of your action):

Outlets / Marketplaces: Amazon, Itunes, Nook, Kobo, Lulu, 24Symbols, Scribd, GooglePlay, HummingbirdDM, etc. - These sell your books for you for a percentage of your royalties.

Aggregators: Smashwords, Lulu, Draft2Digital, StreetLib, PublishDrive – these send your book to these outlets for another percentage of your royalties. But save you time.

Distributors/Wholesalers: Ingrams, OverDrive, Baker & Taylor, American West, etc. - these reach other outlets and mainly deal with hardcopy books. OverDrive can get your ebooks (and audiobooks) into libraries where they are leased on a recurring basis, selling the same book over and over.

Most of these cross over. Most wholesalers have a distributor function (for a much larger piece of your pie.) Aggregators ship to distributors as well as outlets. Lulu has an online catalog (touted as the worlds largest independent bookstore) and is also an aggregator for both digital and print versions. Many aggregators now deal with both ebook and audio.

4. **Open for Headliners** – play in front of multiple audiences to get them to join yours. There is nothing more disheartening than to throw a party or concert where no one shows up. Send your book(s) to places where you can be an also-ran and get discovered. As said above, no one store has all the customers. Get everywhere you can and then use universal links such as Books2Read.com in order to sell to people everywhere you are. Do joint-venture giveaways with other authors to get your books known and appreciated. Better mousetraps don't sell just because they are invented.

6. **Sell to Marketplace Crowds** – the key to selling books is to get other people to sell them for you. Instead of owning a big tent in the middle of the dessert, rent a small booth in a large bazaar where lots of people visit with the idea of buying things.

Look over that list of book outlets and warehouses, and distributors, and aggregators above carefully. They want to sell your book for you. Sure, you could set up a site and then work your tail off getting people to come to you. And you'd routinely make 90% royalties and never have to limit your price. But look at how much you'd have to spend to get people there to buy.

You put your book into existing marketplaces. Outlets are marketplaces. Everyone of those places above either have their own marketplace or ship to places that do. That's the key. They already have audiences you want to get your book(s) in front of.

What people want to sell you is your own storefront in the desert. Watch out for these. Look for somewhere that you can get a booth in their bazaar instead. They'll charge you a bit more (maybe not) in order to be there. Amazon is one of these. So are iTunes, Kobo,

Nook, and the rest. In general, the bigger the marketplace (or more physical the product) the higher your booth rent.

Sure, I sell my own books direct. And make over 90% on each sale when I do. But those sales don't even make a dark spot in the shadows compared to what I get from the established book outlets.

This especially goes for courses. Sure, there is a lot of money to be made in courses, way more than individual books they are based on. The trick is that you can sell your own version from your own site, while other marketplaces are selling your same material for you. Have your cake and eat it, too.

You also want multiple aggregators – most of the well-known aggregators only go to a handful of outlets. StreetLib and PublishDrive get you into European and small U.S. ebook outlets and can make you as much as Amazon for the same set of books. Because they each reach several dozen outlets and leverage the long tail. Always be on the look out for new startups in these areas. Again, no one aggregator can reach all the outlets.

5. **Listen to Conventional Wisdom Carefully – and Go The Other Way.** There is tons of manure out there being peddled as book sales fertilizer. More money was made off the gold miners in any gold rush than was ever taken out of the ground. More courses are being offered every day that all say the same stuff. And that stuff is only partial solutions at best. Most of these places were either vanity publishers or taken their place.

It's true that its easier than ever to publish a book, but the chances of selling enough to make a living has gotten even harder. Amazon, while known as the world's largest single book sales outlet, is also known as the world largest indie author's graveyard as 99.9% of their books ever sell more than a couple hundred books at best – and these are mostly family and friends of the author.

And its true that most authors don't know how to edit, make a cover, or market. So they need some help. But if they'd simply do some Internet research, they'd find the common practices that have been tested and work.

Courses You Can Invest in -

...but don't — until you actually have done your homework.

The sources I mention here I've tested and found to have no-nonsense approaches, and are personally successful from what they teach.

Geoff Shaw's Kindling. Best for the price. Also his Udemy courses are very good (get them when Udemy is running one of their specials.)

Mark Dawson's FB Ads for authors. You can learn the basics from his free videos, and then decide if you want the rest. Lifetime access and updates when you do.

Nick Stephenson's course. A good, solid overview of building a system to support your author career. Get his free books and videos first.

Tim Grahl's course. Most expensive of all of these. And most of his approach can be figured out from his free books.

Theauthoracademy.com – from **C.J. Daniels.** Chunk full of great resources.

Chris Fox – no-nonsense and simple books about how to start from nowhere and create some bestsellers. His 5 books on Kindle are a cheap investment (less than $20) and his videos about these books can be found online or in Daniels' site above.

Amy Collins – plenty of stuff on her newshelves.com site, as well as her courses with Real Fast Marketing. Helps you get into wholesalers to reach Libraries and Indie bookstores.

Look, I've spent a decade doing this. And have only you to tell about it. That's why I'm writing this. My muse told me to do it. Better than having it all forgotten.

If You're Starting From Scratch With No Budget

— here's the breakdown:

- Geoff Shaw's course can be had for about $125. (and get his Udemy courses when they go on sale.)
- Daniels' Academy is about $100.
- Get Dawson's free videos.
- Get Stephenson's free videos.
- Get Grahl's free books.
- Get Fox's books and watch his YouTube videos.

If You Have a Budget, Don't Spend, <u>Invest</u>.

Use your day job to cover your costs, but make sure you treat that as an investment. *Every publishing business should pay its own way.* You probably aren't funded by venture capital (and shouldn't be.)

The heart of any success as an author is to build and run your publishing as a *business*. That means paying back your investment by making your money get returns.

The only failures are people treating it as a hobby and then expecting it to return income like a business. Passive, residual income doesn't mean you do nothing, it means you don't have to create every product. It used to be (like Robert Kiyosaki) that you had to print a few thousand books and sell them from your garage. Now you can set them up to get printed when they are sold. You don't have to print and warehouse and sell your own books. But you do have to get other people to do it for you. And the money you invest in that effort needs to come back to you.

If you buy a course, it should result in at least that many royalties to reimburse you for the costs. Same for any program or tool you buy. Same for any how-to book. Same for the bandwidth you use. Your web hosting should be bringing you income. Get a dollars and sense mindset. *"How will this enable me to earn more income?"* That's your mantra.

The Author Platform

This evolved from Tim Grahl's courses (free and paid) and my own experience. No one ever really defines a "platform." Those that do mainly talk about how well you can market your book, which is only part of it. An author without books can only get pre-sales for so long.

Grahl has a lot of experience in launching single books successfully. He's familiar with two types of authors who hire him: those with a big list (audience) and those with a big network. He missed two other types, although they are both present – those who have a big vision/core idea, and those who have a lot of content.

People like John Jantzch who wrote *Ducktape Marketing*, have a single/core idea and a single book they then produce variations of as well as produce their income from courses, speeches, and coaching. Stephen Covey also did that approach.

Authors who have a lifetime of content can also make a good living. Isaac Asimov was one like this, as well as Napoleon Hill. You probably don't know that Hill made three million-dollar fortunes in his life, publishing dozens of books. You can take Earl Nightingales' Our Changing World radio show with it's nearly 7,000 broadcasts, in addition to his recorded talks. Or Jim Rohn who made his second fortune by recording and re-selling his lectures. Or Al Capp's *Lil' Abner* comic strips, or Watterson's ever popular *Calvin and Hobbes*. Tons of content.

Boil these down, and you'll see a system:

- **Vision** – your ideal you are reaching for, your faith in the inevitable success of your actions.

- **Content** – the ideas you have as published in the various containers you can pour those ideas into.

- **Audience** – people who want what you offer and will pay you for it. This is represented by the size of your mailing list.

- **Network** – people who are in your area of expertise and you have dealt with personally. These are also your affiliate sales people in addition to your doctor, dentist, stockbroker, supermarket check-out person. This is your mastermind group, as well as people you talk to once a year.

In these four points, you see a practical and working definition of what your platform can be, as well as how to grow it.

Look them over and see what you can do to firm up each one.

Most marketing revolves around building your list.

Grahl and Stephenson talk about building and using both audience and network to have successful launches and marketing campaigns for books. Stephenson is talking about having multiple books available for sale, but also attributes his own success to networking with fellow authors, in doing joint launches with them.

But you'll find people who simply got in front of people as a speaker and pitched their book to them (which could be bought as a special discount just for that event, in the back of the room.)

You'll find people who create a course full of data and then sell the textbook as a reference for that course.

And then there are the extreme cases of content publishers who amass a huge list of books which people want to read and arrange to ship their particular order to them. Book of the Month Club was one of these. Dover Publications is another.

- **Vision,**
- **Content,**
- **Audience,**
- **Network.**

When you start working on one, you'll find it builds up the others. That's why it's a system. People buy your books and join your list. You promote your other content to them. Some are authors on their own and can help you with joint venture promotions. But this will succeed to the exact point where you have a strong vision about the result you want.

You can launch using any of these four points, or any combination of them. Grahl has anecdotes of people who did nothing more than tell their network they had a book. Or who only told their list about their book. Any publisher who can navigate the rocky shores of public domain publishing can find safe harbor and financial freedom. (Not for the faint at heart, though.)

You don't have to start big, but you have to start. If you have a small list, a small network, then let them all know about your book. OK, so the first one only sells a couple hundred copies. Most of the big names didn't start making decent income until their fifth book, like J. K. Rowling. She wrote the first three while government welfare payments footed the bills. Finally a publisher picked up her first book, but her career really took off after they published the fifth one. Stephen King had the same deal. His fifth book was the tipping point.

"Write, publish, repeat" is the title for one of the books that describes this scene.

If you just want a NYT bestseller, you can write a book, pay for editing and a cover, then pay an exorbitant amount to have a business buy your books in all the right places and get it onto that list. It will disappear of that list the next week, but you made your target and will ever after be known as a "NYT bestselling author."

Geoff Shaw tells about authors who use multiple pen names and pull down consistent six and seven-figure income without anyone knowing who it really is. And their books sell well, but don't necessarily hit bestseller lists (well, perhaps on Amazon.) Author Earnings' Data Guy confirms that there are still holes in their data gathering where some authors can be represented several times in their data as high-selling, but their pen names aren't able to be consolidated to find out how much they are actually making, much less how they are doing it. That's just tons of content talking at you.

Work From Your Sweet Spot

That brings up the point of working with your strengths.

Joe Pulizzi in his *Content Inc.* mentions the idea of a sweet spot. (His book actually lays out a good business plan for any author-publisher.)

Pulizzi says that there is *what you know* and *what you're trained at doing*. You create your content from the intersection of these two. (And see his book for a deeper explanation. But the idea is simple and should have already turned on a few light bulbs for you.)

This was extended by others to include the audience more. The sweet spot is also *what the audience wants* and *what they will pay you for*.

Draw that up in a Venn diagram with overlapping circles of interest and influence and you'll then see that the center of all of these is where you can write and publish to.

Compare that with Chris Fox's *Write to Market*, as well as Shaw's material, and you'll see that it's all the same content.

You have to write what you like to read, and you have to sensibly write in genres which are selling.

And if you want to wonk out on those genres, you can study the free PDF's and video's which k-lytics.com produces monthly.

You can write books which will sell in any genre. But how much you want to earn from your writing will depend on your own vision. And that might determine which genre you want to write in. Keep in mind that your writing should be a joy. If you want to make a huge income, then it's still that you write the books you like to read, just narrow down to the type which people are buying lots of them. Instead of cat mysteries, you might need to move over to cozy mysteries, or women detectives. All of these sub-sub-genres sell, it's just that some sell better than others. More readers looking for those books.

Social Networks Warnings

In general, *avoid*. Syndicate your posts to them but don't spend your time there. Use Facebook to run ads to people who do. Because the social networks are set up to limit access to the amount of organic followers you have, in favor of your paying to reach them. Tim Grahl and others found that authors in general don't sell many books there, especially compared to the time you invest/waste.

IFTTT.com (If This Then That) will do your syndication to almost anywhere. (Zapier can do this too, but it will cost you to do it with any volume at all.)

Spend your time writing and marketing instead, which includes building your list and directly communicating with them. Those are real conversations with people who have bought your books.

The few exceptions would be LibraryThing and Goodreads, maybe Wattpad. Because these are social networks for book lovers. And the uber-readers (more than one book per week) are constantly looking for people with lists of books to read. LibraryThing also has librarians there, who might stock your book for you. And libraries are where these uber-readers go for print versions as well as ebooks.

The point is that you can't get a return of _time_ *from investment, only* _money_. Don't fritter your time on "liking" or "tweeting" cat pictures when you should be writing or marketing. Instead, write and market a *book* on cat pictures *if* you find there's a viable market for it.

Lack of Links

Sorry, but this was an inspired brain-dump. It's missing all sorts of links. The sites I've mentioned above can all be found simply by Google search. You can access all of the outlets, aggregators, and wholesalers to set up accounts for publishing your books through them. Most of the wholesalers and distributors would prefer you act like a "grown-up" (bona-fide) publisher rather than an author with a book to pitch. So get a dozen books before you start submitting to them. You might go ahead and publish some friend's books for them while you're at it. CDBaby.com and (later) Bookbaby.com actually started this way.

Takeaways

1. Publish everywhere you can in all formats you can. Diversify.

2. Invest in publishing as a business, not a hobby. Make your business support itself. Get your money (and time) to pay back that investment.

3. Find and work from your sweet spot.

4. Build your platform and work from your strengths. You can make a living by having a single book, or you can write hundreds. Whatever turns your crank.

Wishing you every success you can earn.

II - Win - Place - Show and the Two Print-On-Demand Races

There's a lot of promotion going around about the various Print on Demand (POD) publishing outlets.

And the one thing that is true about Conventional Wisdom is that it's usually false.

I've used Lulu since 2006 and that isn't about to change. This was before Ingram and Createspace got into the game.

The main two reasons: cost and quality.

Most people omit Lulu when they talk about POD. To them, its a two-horse race. For me, there is one horse who wins the sprints, one horse who wins the long haul, and an also-ran that merely places behind the other two.

Here's the Also-Ran: IngramSpark.

Short review: Goes everywhere you want to show up. Highly recommended by the pundits.

Set up cost for each book: $49.

Annual distribution fee: $12 (or it drops out of their catalog and you have to start over.)

(Each) revision fee: $25

Note: don't bother with putting your ebook up there. You have to take it down elsewhere, in general. Use al the other aggregators you can to get it everywhere you can.

Sprint Winner: CreateSpace

Short review: Great for cheap copies inside Amazon, lousy anywhere else.

You don't have to pay the 55% distribution costs to get into Amazon that everyone else has. So your CreateSpace paperback is cheaper. And they produce most of the sizes that IngramSpark can do for you.

No set up costs. No annual distribution fee. No revision fee. You can get your print book up the day as your ebook on Kindle, and they will both get approved about the same time.

On their extended distribution - don't bother. There are no returns and your book has an Amazon stigma attached to it. Most Indie bookstores, distributors and B&N won't accept a CreateSpace paperback. And you'll have to raise your price to enable that 55%, or take a huge drop in your royalty. Welcome to the big track, not just the inside track.

Long Haul Winner: Lulu

Short review: Set up costs - none. You have to buy a proof at their costs. But you get a copy in your hands, which is satisfying. Revision costs - another proof. (Yes, you pay shipping, but Lulu is always running some discount or other.) Annual distribution fee - none. Your book stays on Ingram from there on out.

Most of the "independent" reviews of Lulu tack on all sorts of imaginary costs and fees. In actuality, the real costs of printing are that proof you have in your hands. And that is only if you want expanded distribution. Anyone who pays for covers and editing always has that cost. Just like CreateSpace or IngramSpark.

The bottom line is that they do it cheaper than anyone who can get you into global distribution in print. And no one else does print and ebooks from the same interface.

Lulu publishes the three most commonly accepted printing sizes for distribution: trade paperback (6x9), letter size (8.5x11), square (8.5x8.5 - but color interior only.)

Other book version notes:

Lulu and IngramSpark do hardbacks, Create Space doesn't.

Lulu ships your ebook to the major ebook outlets, as long as it's original. They'll convert it for you as well.

IngramSpark only takes PDF files for print books. Lulu and Createspace take several types of documents.

Why This Matters for Self-Publishing Authors:

Anyone has overhead when you're running your business as a business and not as a hobby. Successful authors will have 30-40 or more books up there for their career. I've heard many are north of 90. (I'm at several dozen dozen and rising, but not in all formats.) You want to diversify your sales as not everyone wants a Kindle ebook, and Amazon can be fickle at times. I get more sales on average from paperbacks than anything else. You want to have audiobook versions, and maybe a course if your book is non-fiction.

Lulu is pretty much set and forget. You have your proof and can simply start marketing your book. It is available everywhere Ingram goes, forever. You can have your ebook, hardback, paperback all from the same content. There are other aggregators for ebooks than Lulu who can get you farther and even with better royalties, but not many.

Createspace also does CD's. Think: spoken word albums. But you won't get your book widely accepted everywhere, and they have had occasional print quality problems.

Ingram does ebooks, paperbacks, and hardbacks. But you can't revise without costs, you have to pay for all your books to remain in distribution every single year. Not much, but don't miss that notice...

Booksales income is passive, but it's not *set-and-forget-about-it*. Mostly, anyway. If you want to pay extra for stuff, go right ahead. Meanwhile, there are many service providers who will take your book and get it onto IngramSpark for you with all the extra's you can afford.

Or you can to the work yourself and get started today. And not worry about extra costs at every turn.

That's why I've stuck with Lulu for a decade and don't see changing anytime soon.

III - A Workflow and Roadmap for Book Production

There are efficient ways to get things done, and time-wasters.

An overall schedule, roughly based on Stephen King's "On Writing" is:

AM - Writing

Aft - Marketing/Business

PM - Reading

You read in order to train and inspire yourself to write. Evenings help to prime your muse, and the early am, right after sleep, is the best time to harvest that inspiration (and keeping a notepad by your bedside to keep track of ideas that wake you up in the darkness.

We Need To Leverage All Our Assets

Two points to review:

1. Books as Idea Containers
2. Multiple Eyeball Publishing.

Books aren't just print or ebooks or audio. They are all of them. And they are videos and courses as well. Maybe even movies and Broadway productions, but that might be extreme hoping.

You actually want to publish in all possible versions to all possible outlets simultaneously. If you want to practice leaving money on the table, just stick to Kindle ebooks. That Amazon route *requires* you to regularly produce content (a new novel at least every three months) and probably run advertising as well to keep your books ranking. In short, you are feeding the beast.

The alternative is to work the long tail and get your books selling in hundreds of local ebook outlets, indie book stores and libraries. More eyeballs seeing your books will result in more sales. Being on a single outlet who only shows the topselling books will not get your book notices. Have your books show up where the others aren't can get you sales that the others don't know they are missing.

For example, Kobo sells better in Canada (and a few other countries) that Amazon. European countries are still starting to find ebooks, and there are a lot of indie ebook companies starting up out there (as well as in the U.S.) Another place is to get your books into libraries, and there are companies who will lease your book to them and then resell your book regularly as they can lend them only so many times. And this includes your audiobooks as well.

Warning: *This is a roadmap for <u>prolific</u> authors.* If you love to write, you shouldn't hold yourself back because Amazon won't reward you for being prolific. This system is tested and works. You won't find this being written up elsewhere, as most people are stuck on how "hard" it is to get their first book out.

This particular book and this particular chapter in it are designed to let you soar your production and ignore the also-rans around you that are drinking the Kool-Aid.

What we will be covering here can open your eyes or make you throw this book across the room.

You can produce four books a week and have the weekend off. You will be producing these in about 7 formats and publishing them as close to simultaneously as possible.

This makes you income as you put your books onto every possible marketplace you can so that they will sell your books for you.

While everyone else if fretting and worrying over their Amazon sales, you can be everywhere else in addition to Amazon, and be hauling in nets of income, fishing in waters where others haven't even heard of.

It begins by working out how to create all possible versions of your book simply and efficiently, then working out how to send your book everywhere others aren't. This diversifies your income and makes a sudden drop by any one outlet to be an inconvenience, not a disaster.

How to Create All Possible Formats Froma A Single Idea - <u>Production</u> Workflow

I've gone over a rough version in this book of all the various types (ebook, print, audio, video, courses) and the big names of outlets, aggregators, distributors, and wholesalers.

The trick is to get these produced in a simple format that doesn't duplicate your efforts.

In "Backwards Book Publishing" I covered that non-fiction should best be done from the course backwards. You talk the book, transcribe/edit the text, marry the text with the images to have the videos. That results in your text, audio, and video in the same effort.

It's efficient, effective, and *way* more profitable than ebooks only.

This Barebones Production Workflow Is:

1. Outline your content.

2. Create a presentation based on your outline, include images that help get your points across.

3. Talk your presentation and record your content.

4. Edit your audio into shape (removing the ah's, uh's, dead spaces) and submit to a transcription service.

5. Extract the slides as images and combine these with the audio as a video.

6. Send out for transcript. At this point, you could upload the video as a private version to YouTube and Google will transcribe it for you, without punctuation. But it's free. Otherwise, I recommend Trint.com as most cost and time efficient for the money you invest. See that book above for a discussion on transcription services.

6. Split the video into lessons in editing your videos for the course.

7. As you edit the transcript, you'll build your text-based book versions.

The reason for doing this is that speaking your book is 3-5 times faster than writing. And editing your transcript saves you a draft overall (which I'll get to later.)

As you start this workflow, your audio won't match the book and might have to be re-edited. Maybe not. Those might be bonuses which make the audio even more authentic.

At about 150 words per minute, a 15K-word book like Chris Fox's non-fiction books will wind up roughly 100 minutes or 1 hour, 40 minutes. Since print books are somethind around 300 words per page (Amazon says 250 words is a "page" on Kindle), then this is roughly a 1:2 or 3:5 ratio wpm/words-per-page. Shorthand is to say that 2 minutes of talking equals one print page. 15K-word book gives you 50 pages in print.

On a course, the standard is 3-5 minute videos, so a hundred minutes will give you 20 videos or more. Depending on your structure, if you do 5 videos per module, then you have 4 modules. The more precise strategy would be to build the videos as four acts, then record short intro and summary videos about half the time of the main acts. So: 5 videos per module. But you'll have to work your book into these formats so you aren't doing an uninspired drudgery of going back to record the small bits for each module. Consider the modern TV "beat" method of having a teaser, then four acts, then a cliffhanger for the next episode. Makes your non-fiction quite more engaging when you think and write it through in those models.

The point is to have your text, audio, and video all ready at the beginning so that your content shows up in all possible outlets in all possible formats. After that, you can figure out how to launch it.

A sidebar here: if you are completely unknown as an author, and just learning your craft, you're probably going to want to work with Short Reads (covered in my two books *"How to Write Less and Profit More"* and *"Writing Serial Fiction in the Real World"*.) Publish 4 to 8 short stories and/or short reads and then collect these up into a bigger book which can be profitably advertised. It's possible to write a short story/read every week, and then release/launch a collection every 5th or 9th/10th week. If none of your stories sell, then you've had that much practice. If you shoot at 10k words per story/episode, then you'll wind up with a novella in the collection. In four to five months. you'd have a 80K-word book, or about 266-page book. If your short stories aren't selling, you can revamp your stories and start a new series. Rinse, iterate, repeat. Better than writing an 80K novel and burning a third of a year with nothing to show for it. Meanwhile, if those short stories/reads do sell, then you have some income while you write the rest of them. And getting feedback from your readers meanwhile. I've gone over this several times in various books and blog posts, but it bears repeating as Conventional Wisdom Kool-Aid drinkers ignore this workflow.

Organizing Your Efficient <u>Publishing</u> Workflow.

At this point you have all the versions, now it's time to work out a publishing sequence. What follows is mostly for non-fiction, but can be adapted for fiction, especially if you sell your book as a video as well. I mean, why not?

Back to the beginning:

0. **Have a site, domain name, and a blog.** Simple is best. Get a Blogger blog and Gumroad to get started. Cheapest and most stable. Set up a landing page for your book as somewhere to send people. Just blank is fine for now. We'll build this as we go. (There are some great themes for Blogger these days...)

00. **Get an email service.** A lot of people like MailChimp. Regardless, you'll be paying something per month or per quarter just to be able to broadcast to subscribers. Gumroad will allow you to email your customers directly, but you'll want to be able to set up a sequence of emails in an autoresponder sequence (like a free ecourse) as well as the occasional or regular email broadcast.

I. Building Your Book

00. **Build an empty book in Calibre** and enter all the metadata, as well as getting the cover made. This includes both long and short description, also you keywords, title, and subtitle. Update your site landing page with this data.

0. **Storyboard your work**. Take some looseleaf notebook paper (the ones with the pre-punched holes so you can put

them into a binder) and draw a box on the top half. Then sketch into it your idea of what picture represents what you're going to talk about.

Below that, you outline what you want to say about that picture.

1. **When you have all the storyboards in place, go through them once or twice to tell that story.** At first you stop and add or rearrange the pages so they make best sense. Once you have it all in order, then time the next run-through. Now you know approximately how many minutes/words/pages you'll have as a result. Trim or expand or simply record.

2. **Edit your recording** to take out the uh's, ah's, and deadspaces.

3. **Make a presentation out of your storyboards.** Get the images you want there.

4. **Export these slides as images.**

5. **Combine with the audio into a video editor** and tweak until the video comes out the way you want it.

(An alternative is to simply screen capture your recording the presentation, then edit the video. Extract the audio to upload for your transcript.)

6. **Upload your audio to get your transcript**. Draft One.

7. **Open up LibreOffice and convert your transcript into a book.** Put in the headings and bullet points and dress it up so it reads well. Add in all the links and correct the grammar and typo's -> Draft Two.

8. **Create your PDF and use that to proof your book**. Tweak, re-export, re-proof. Final Draft, print copy is now ready.

9. **Output with Calibre to epub** and check this with its editor. (Or use Writer2Epub plug-in for LibreOffice.)

10. **When you're happy with the result, have Calibre create a mobi version.**

- - - -

II. Publishing and Producing Your Book

1. **Publish your courses to Udemy**, Skillshare, and the other course marketplaces. Create any needed PDF handouts to match the videos, and link to your site for more information. If you have a built-in LMS (Learning Management System) on your site, great. Build your course there as well. Or build it there first to get the bugs out.

2. **Publish your audio to Author's Republic and CD Baby.** Integrate Gumroad on your site so you can sell your digital versions there - starting with the audiobook.

3. **Publish to Lulu.** This gives you free ISBN's for each book. Ebook is for Lulu only, we'll send to other outlets shortly. Paperback goes to "globalReach" (Expanded Distribution) while you hold on to your hardback until you like what you see in the paperback proof (cheaper, obviously.) Those proofs take about a week or so to get to you, so...

4. **Publish to CS as Paperback and audio CD**, even individual videos can be sold. DVD if you have the chops to produce one. (No, we won't publish to Kindle until much later. Follow my logic on this one...)

5. **ebook to Draft2Digital** (originals only, no public domain.) They have merchandizing capability and specials you can't easily access otherwise. That gets you to iTunes, Kobo, Nook, and a few others. This also gives you a universal link so that people can buy wherever they prefer.

6. **ebook to StreetLib and PublishDrive**. These two aggregators gets your book into Europe, as well as most of the rest of the major US and worldwide outlets.

7. **At this point, set up your digital sales on Gumroad** (epub, mobi, and PDF as a bundle) and link those into your Book post on Blogger. Once you get a few of these, you can create your bundles, and also send people directly to your personal Gumroad site as well. Don't forget you can set up your audio book on Gumroad for direct sales and then make a bundle with the ebook package.

III. Publishing to Kindle

Finally, your Kindle version is different than your other ebooks.

Because Amazon has set it up that way to make as much profit as possible. There's all sorts of tricks built into their system which people have figured out almost as fast as Amazon can fix them.

This means you need to make a special edition for Kindle which has an opt-in link that shows up in the LookInside, plus your usual pitch at the back of your book, and a host of other details. Amazon has been dissected to death on how to best create ebooks for it, plus the keywords and so forth. So there is no repeating all those hacks here.

You do this last, so you can take advantage of things like pre-orders and a few other Kindle-centric marketing strategies.

Again, it's one ebook for everyone else and then a special edition for Amazon. Amazon is priced lower (because they'll nag you if they aren't) and you can do all sorts of launch strategies with them. Those books tell all about this. Chris Fox has probably the best book (with his video series as well) about launching there.

The reason I say to do this last is because every where else is pretty much set-and-forget. But Amazon throws your book off another financial cliff every 30 days where your sales tank unless you constantly push traffic to them with ads. So you have to treat them special kid gloves. Of course, they reward you with extreme payouts if you do it just right. And that means people get sucked up in gaming Amazon's algorithms.

The other alternative is to simply keep cranking out books and seeing which series sells everywhere else as well. I've found that the books which sell at all sell everywhere without having to get reviews for Amazon or advertise. Amazon is its own animal. Another author has told me he gets as many sales from long-tail distribution as he does from Amazon. And he doesn't advertise. He also doesn't do audiobooks or courses, just ebooks and print books. So there is a lot still to gain here.

You'll have to approach this on your own. Almost all of the conventional wisdom these days is Amazon-centric. But if you can make as much income from the international book sales not on Amazon as on it, then that's saying something. Meanwhile, you aren't running around doing all you have to do in order to get sales just on Amazon. You can then just enjoy writing and work on improving your craft. That's what passive income is all about – less work, more income, more free time to do what you want.

This strategy says that to survive best, get as many versions of your books out to every book outlet you can find. Publish them all at once, then start on the next book.

The theory of "4 shorts and a collection" is an Amazon workaround. Books sell better when they are advertised (on Facebook and on Amazon) and when you have at least a $3.99 unit price to pay for that advertising. You put up the four short reads/stories once a week or every two weeks as a series. They will tend to promote the other books in that series on Amazon. Then you come out with a collection that initially sells for .99 and then raises slowly. Of course, you build your list and segment that list so the least responsive are alerted about a new release first, then the next most-responsive, and until you've mailed your entire list. This is to set up your book for regular sales and convince Amazon its worth their while to promote your book for the next month. Again, see Fox's book, Launch to Market, for details.

Amazon is a beast and you don't want to have to be feeding it all the time. That's just another job with no benefits.

You want to write in genres where you like writing and make income without having to jump through hoops to get there.

If you do decide to create an Amazon solopreneur business like Mark Dawson, then you have that marketing time slot available - afternoons.

Your choice.

IV. In Short:

a. Create your book in all possible formats - text, audio, video.

b. Publish your course.

c. Publish your audio and video's.

d. Publish your print books.

e. Publish your ebooks.

f. Publish your Kindle ebook.

g. Rinse, repeat.

IV - How to Train Yourself To Speak Your Fiction Book

This isn't simple, as it's not intuitive. We aren't an oral culture these days. And there weren't audio books to record in those days. Now anyone with a computer can record. The time is right to re-learn these skills.

Most of the guides and texts on authorship have to do with writing. But writing is probably less normal than speaking. The proof of this is that speaking is a faster creation process than writing.

We just aren't used to it.

Look, the average person speaks about 150 words per minute. In an hour, this is 9000 words.

The fastest typist on record, with a special keyboard, can only match that speed. The average writer does between 500 and 2,000 words per hour. Chris Fox and others can get this upwards of 5,000 words per hour.

Now, Fox's method includes not stopping for corrections, including backspacing. So you have another day of editing, which means out of around two days, you have 2500 usable words per hour.

Audio is several times faster, but you'll then go and edit your audio to remove the errors and dead space. That action takes at least as much time as recording. The transcription is the next step, which is another cost and added time to get it back (or use Trint.com to get it back the same day. Record an hour, edit that audio, fix the transcription. Three days of this and you'll have 27,000 usable words and a 90-page first draft. At current prices, that is about $45 in cost to get your text and also have a working audiobook.

That's the trick, above the faster speed possible to anyone with out special training. You can create additional streams of income from the same central idea.

The usual sequence of writing is:

1. Write out the first draft.

2. Go back through and fix obvious continuity errors while you put in links - second draft.

3. Do a line edit and fix each sentence on it's own - third draft.

4. Talk your book out loud and correct the phrasing - fourth draft.

5. Record that fourth draft and edit it, and you have your audio book.

6. Send the fourth draft out for proofing.

Now, speaking your book cuts at least one draft out of this.

Talk your book, edit the audio. Edit your own transcription on Trint.com - you're now at the second draft.

Line edit and put in the links. Third draft, ready for proofing.

Of course, I'm shorthanding the editing of this book. And also the learning curve of hiring a developmental editor to take you through your own learning to write fiction.

On the other hand, you can simply post your stories up to Wattpad for feedback.

25K-word stories once a week. After a few of these, you'll have a base of stories that you can publish, based on the corrections you did after feedback.

The Secret to Learning To Talk Stories.

Read out loud.

Yes, that's the trick. Find short stories in the area you want to write in. Read these out loud to yourself each night (or to your children.) This is one of the ways of learning, much like copywriters would take other's ads and hand write them in order to internalize the patterns they used in those ads.

Get collections of short stories in your genre and read them out loud every night. Then go through and dissect them according to the Story Grid for the plot elements and how they were used. Get the most popular short stories on Gutenberg and fill up a notebook with dissecting each story.

You can then outline a story based on that plot dissection and speak it out.

Commonplacebook [http://commonplacebook.com/writing/word-counts-of-famous-short-stories/] holds the average at about 4K words, which is about 27 minutes.

Word counts on full fiction works start at about 80K on average, and can run upwards of 120K. [http://theswivet.blogspot.com/2008/03/on-word-counts-and-novel-length.html]

When you take this backwards to construct your book, let's apply that teaser/four acts/cliffhanger above. teaser and cliffhanger total to another act. So you'll need to do about 5 minutes for each act. 2.5, 5, 5, 5, 5, 2.5. 5 x 150 is 750 words. Totals about 25 minutes or over 18000 words, which is over 60 pages in print.

Talk in 5 minute sections. But how to plot these?

Storyboarding For Fun And Profit

I'm graphic by nature, so let's try the Disney storyboard concept. Take your story outline (plot dissection) from the short story you read and worked over.

Per Story Grid, each beat, scene, sequence, act, sub-plot, and global story has five points:

1. Inciting Incident

2. Progressive Complication

3. Crisis

4. Climax

5. Resolution

For that TV script, you can have the teaser as the incident, and the cliffhanger as a sixth step which is the inciting incident for the next episode. That gives you four acts and 2 half-acts. And so you can then create your acts with the 5 minutes of talking for each act.

Back to dissection. Your 4K short story could be broken down (in theory) to 5 parts with an average of 800 words per section (m/l).

Lay those out in your word processor and see how they fit in. Look over the sentences and how they build to each part they need.

Then storyboard those stories to see what scenes they entail, and actions, as well as actor reactions. See how many images you need to communicate those different scenes, actions, and reactions. (Note: Geoff Shaw has a different layout, based on Evan Marshall's "*Marshall Plan for Novel Writing*". And Blake Snyder's "*Save the Cat*" covers this differently as well. Lester Dent had an assembly line approach for a 6K word story. [http://www.paper-dragon.com/1939/dent.html]

The point is to work up your story within those word counts and minutes. After you've storyboarded a few of these, the pattern will emerge. You're going to do this for the rest of your writing career, so it should get easier with time.

Take one of the plots you've outlined and storyboard your own characters and settings into them. Then tell the story that comes to you. You could keep a timer running (no alarm, please) to see if you're going overboard on your time. If you're going to tell the story at one go, then make some time notations on the upper corner to see when you should be turning that page. Again, this is a rough outline of how to train yourself to tell stories against a clock.

The trick is to start with stories which are meant to be told aloud. Some books like Marie Shedlock's *The Art of the Storyteller* and Mark Twain's *How to Tell a Story and Other Essays* have sample stories told to children. Take these, read them aloud, break them down into parts, storyboard them, then build your own story based on that plot with different devices and so on.

The point of this is to work out a method which is simpler, faster, and more efficient than writing. This involves learning skills which you've neglected.

And all this needs a nice, resounding test. I've laid out the broad strokes in the back of this book so you could see if it makes sense to you and then test it for yourself. I'm moving over to fiction myself, and have a stack of books and videos to dissect. But the steps to move over into talking a book have to be re-learned. Creating storyboards should help.

The reason this came up is a logical extension to what I've been covering with the Backwards Book Publishing idea, and extending this into a way people can train themselves to talk a book out.

The Efficiency Test - Does This Work?

The idea is to crank out a short story/read every week, and a collection on the fifth week.

At 4K words per short story, you need about 25 minutes to record it, that much time again (at least) to edit it, and over that much to create the transcript. So in two hours, you could create 4K word short story up to the point (perhaps) that it would be ready for proofing. Your outlining and storyboarding would be outside of that time. Maybe another hour, probably created the night before.

That is one story per day. Amazon only needs 2500 words minimum for a short read (10 pages) and your 4k words would be 16 pages. Four days of this would give you four stories, and a cumulative 16K words at about 54 pages in print (64 Kindle pages.) Four weeks of this would give you a 200-word book, about 64K words, somewhere between a novella and a minimal novel. Again, publish a Kindle short-read and thin paperback on CreateSpace every week of four stories. The fifth week you come out with the collection on Kindle and a paperback thick enough to be a respectable library book.

To meet an 80K/260-page print novel standard, you'd then have to do 20 4K short stories, which is 5 weeks of work at that rate. Your sixth week publishes the complete novel.

Lets compare this to your hour show on TV:

Average hour-long drama is actually about 42 minutes, owing to commercial breaks.

Meaning their acts are something around 8-9 minutes each.

Teasers and cliffhangers are then about 2-4 minutes (Opening teaser goes into credits for another minute, maybe.)

150 wpm would give us (yes, I know, this isn't dialogue or monologue. This is the author describing the scene) - 1200 to 1350 words spoken for each act. The entire show is about 6300 words.

An entire show is at the upper end of what a short story tops out at.

We are basing this on 25 minutes of talking, or 4K words. That is essentially a half-hour show on TV. Mostly good for comedies.

40 minutes of recording would then give us an hour-long dramatic TV episode. In audio books, the breaks between chapters would be the commercial breaks. Start with 25 - 30 minutes of recording and then ramp it up to 40 minutes to enable your listener to take advantage of their propensity to have an "hour-long" drama. (And if you podcast this, you'd simply put your own ads in those locations.)

An interesting point is that some of these shows used progressively shorter acts as the story progressed, so the first act was 12, the second was 8-9, the third was 7 or 8, the fourth was 5-6, and the cliffhanger might stretch to five minutes. (Teasers were a couple of minutes plus credits.)

In these days and age, this might be a formula readers and listeners could agree with.

How Do You Do Video With Fiction?

We covered how to publish everywhere with everything, and that's fine for non-fiction. If you have a graphic artist on tap (or love to spend time picking out photo's) then you could simply set these up to tell their story. A presentation would then just morph into a story telling scene for you. Otherwise, if you have dramatic reading skills (with few errors) then you could simply record yourself with a headshot.

But otherwise, don't sweat it. With fiction, you are working the story into audio and text at the same time. If you can work out how to do video (like some of us cartoonists have no problem cranking out multi-paneled 'toons) then fine.

The point of having videos for non-fiction courses is more the priority. Once you train yourself to create your stories and talk them into existence, then you're set to go. Volume work.

Again, with Amazon's limits, you could write one book and publish it in one series, then another book in a different series the next week. By ten weeks, you'll have tested two genres (maybe with two pen names) and still have your weekends off. If you have two hits, then you've generated some income for most of those weeks and can follow up with another ten weeks of production.

The main point to all of this is to quickly get a lot of content up there that people can buy your backlist. We've just gone over a system where you can create four short stories a week and a 200-page printed collection in four. Sure, it's a full life, but you're watching movies or reading books every night, and have your weekends to do whatever.

Now on a part-time schedule, you may only get a couple of short stories out each week, but if your dream is to write, you are on your way.

All you have to do is to learn to talk your book...

V - Self-Publishing: How to Avoid the Greedy, Ruthless Bully

Conventional Wisdom Says Amazon is the Best Thing that Happened to Self Publishing.

As usual, Conventional Wisdom is completely wrong. Time to turn around and go another way.

I'm no fan of Amazon. I'm not their enemy either. I can see that as a business, they have every right to do what they want. People who sell only there are completely the effect of Amazon's business decisions. And it's a bit like losing all your images that you posted to MySpace, or moaning about the fact that your Facebook followers see less than 10% of your posts these days.

Building on rented land is suicidal, or at least a mild form of self-torture.

Mark Coker has it straight in his 2017 predictions. His Smashwords has been around as long as the Kindle. So he's got some weight to sling around.

Here's the main points:

- Amazon is forcing a race to the bottom among self-publishing authors.
- Ebooks are becoming a cheap commodity.
- More and more authors are finding their best sales days are behind them.
- The changes Amazon is making in their KDP Select and KDP Unlimited have the company's best interests at heart, not the authors'.
- Amazon is getting riper for lawsuit and government regulation as they continue to expand control of the ebook publishing arena.

These are facts. Coker laid them out well and I don't need to review them here.

It's like you have to get by a greedy bully in the self-publishing schoolyard who demands a big part of your lunch money. The bully doesn't care about you. He's getting rich by setting the rules you have to follow. No, we don't know why the teachers let the bully get away with it. But it's only a matter of time before something snaps.

Let's back up here. I've got more pleasant solutions to talk about.

The Tests I've Done Say the Gold Fields Aren't All on Amazon

I've been self-publishing since 2006 and have constantly done tests to understand and poke holes in every book-selling marketplace I can find. And I've got a lot of tests running right now.

During that time, I've seen Amazon go from 90% of the ebook book sales down to nearly 50% and now back up to 70%. And there are some people who are making north of a million dollars annual income mostly from just Amazon ebooks and Facebook ads.

But guess what? Amazon and Facebook own those platforms. You're just sharecropping there. Whatever they change affects your income. And they can cancel your account at any time - and infrequently have.

My early tests showed that I was making a decent income (enough to quit my last day job) on all the sites *other* than Amazon before I started having any decent bestseller there.

And I've seen the Internet Marketing "Gurus" come and go, and try to master the Amazon ebook craze. Some succeeded, most failed. Because Amazon would change their algorithms and the Get Rich Quick guys would go bust.

The ebook-only income model is dead.

What Amazon is Doing Isn't Evil Rocket Science

It's called **leverage**. Look, they started with selling hardcopy books, as this was dead simple and easy for them to get into. Then they expanded into ebooks and used the "buy it here cheaper than anyone else" approach. Then they simply used computers and their own AI to work out how to always sell cheaper.

Unfortunately, this started an automatic "race to the bottom." Their first actions were to automate reviews and so get a clear "social authority" for those books. The problem is that the reviews they get suck as they've been gamed so many times. People don't use reviews by actual study, and they don't leave reviews (unless you email them constantly to get them to do so.) Most of the online booksellers don't utilize reviews as any major scene. Amazon has this plugged into their algorithm somehow, and they push this when they talk to authors.

Reviews and their other algorithms are simply their way to commoditize and mechanize sales. The unintended result of this is that authors themselves tend to be treated as commodities. In the old days of serfs and kings, this was also known as slavery. Authors feel compelled to under-price their books and regularly drop the price for short periods and then spend money to promote when the four-dollar book is at 1 dollar or free. Your sales then *cost* you money.

The traditional publishers actually make more sense at this. eBooks may be cheaper to produce, but they still have to be written and the author needs to be paid. So the traditional publishers tend to set those prices at the same as the paperback. Wouldn't you rather be paid 70% of ten bucks rather than 70% of four bucks?

Especially as most new books only sell 250 copies at best.

We've Passed Peak Ebook Consumption, and Are Due for A Slump

To understand ebook sales, you have to look at Gartner's Hype Curve.

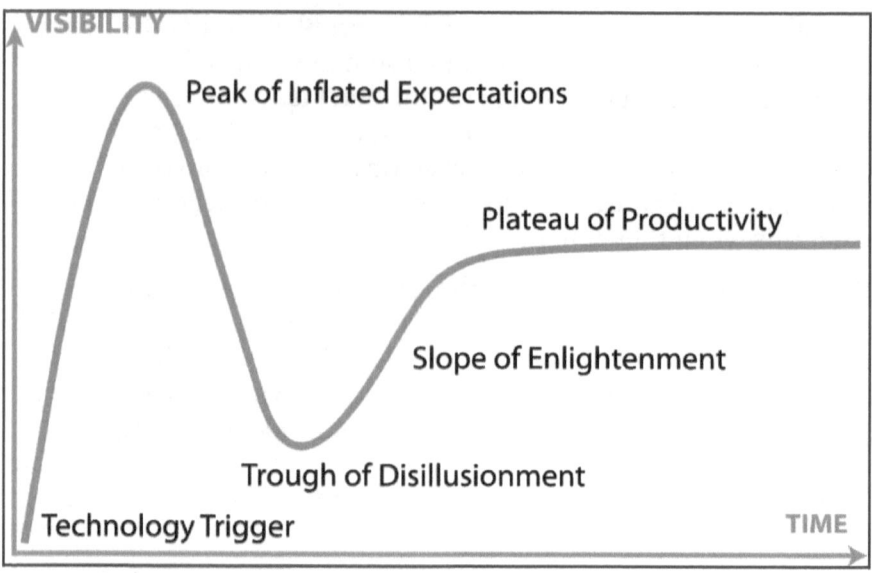

(from Wikipedia)

This is how the scene goes with new technology. When you read Coker's article, it would seem that many authors have hit this Disillusionment stage and are quitting because their ebook income has dropped and it's not as easy to earn income as they thought it should be. Note that Coker's users are primarily ebook authors.

You'll also see in Author Earnings last report that ebooks are starting to dive from indie authors, but increasing from small publishers.

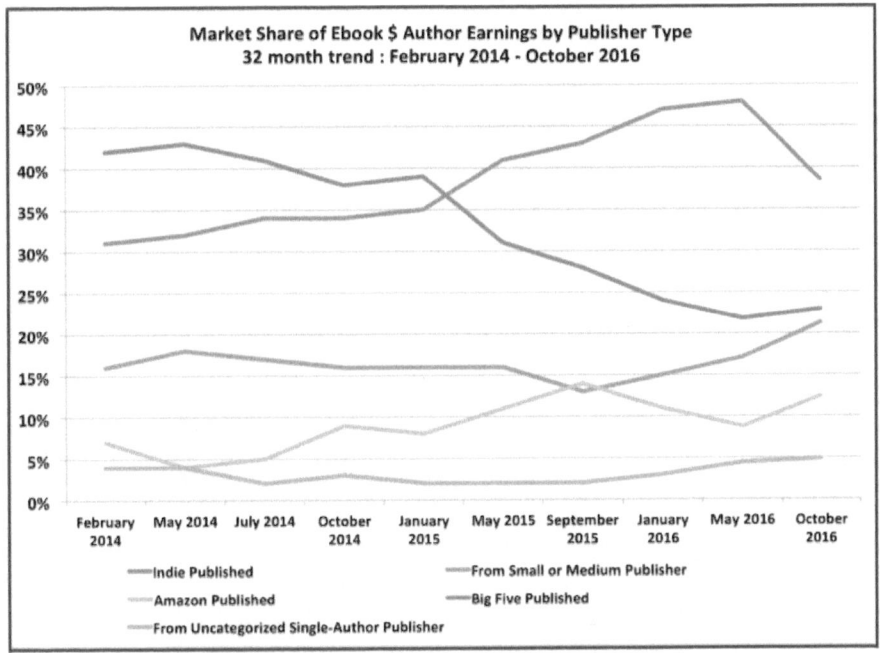

Market Share of Ebook $ Author Earnings by Publisher Type
32 month trend : February 2014 - October 2016

(from http://authorearnings.com/report/october-2016/)

This tends to support Coker's point that indie authors have quit finding it easy to generate income from ebooks alone. Also, perhaps, that Amazon's crunch on the Get Rich Quick Marketers has gotten some effect, and those scammy/spammy marketers are now looking elsewhere for their fast bucks.

The other point is that the small publishers have figured out how to promote ebooks to make them popular. Their low overhead and start-up economy has taken away sales from the Big 5, who depend on big name authors to keep them afloat with all their legacy inefficiencies.

But the real trick is to see the Hype Cycle overlaid on the Bell Curve of technology adoption:

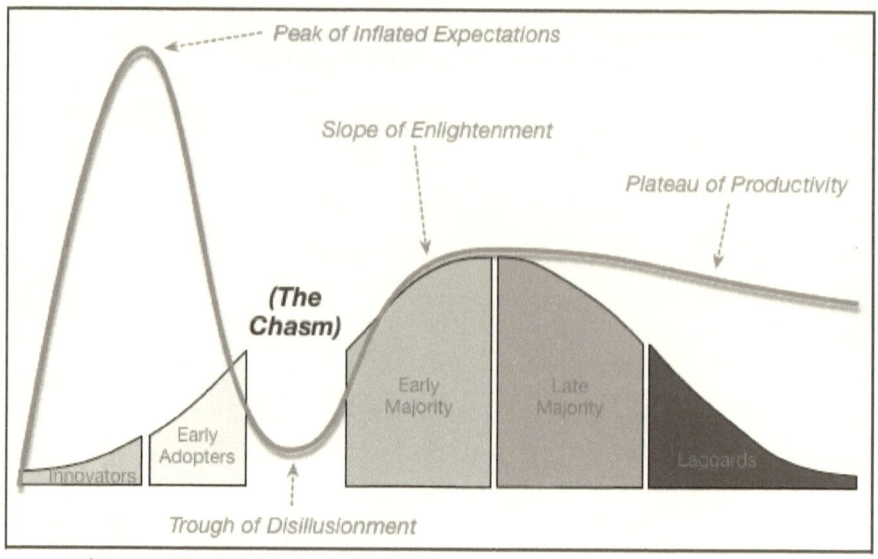

(Tom Graves:
https://www.linkedin.com/pulse/technology-adoption-technology-evolution-tom-graves)

What you may be seeing is that the "easy money" for solo indie-authors has dissipated. So they are leaving the push of trying to earn income from Amazon, or simply hiring or forming small press publishers to have a supporting team that can properly promote their books and achieve a critical mass enough to support their lifestyle.

This is probably a weeding out which was eventual. Amazon already weeds out non-productive books to the bottom of their recommendations, available only really by direct search of that exact title. Authors who can't make sales have been weeding themselves out already. It's evolving to mean that only publishing businesses (even it's a one-person show) will make any regular income from Amazon ebooks. You can't simply publish and hope any more, if ever.

Ebooks still remain about 30% of the total book sales, while print (other than the fad of coloring books) has remained steady to slightly down. Meanwhile, audio books has had a huge uptick and is taking a larger share.

By the above, you could estimate that ebooks have hit their max, where the market is so glutted with new books that discovery has become relatively impossible. Look for ebooks to remain about this level or shrink overall. It depends on where you see them on the curves above. Only having a team behind you and running effective and remunerative ads along with other promotion will allow you to get Amazon's attention with sales so that they will push your book. Everyone else (millions of books) are in the ebook graveyard, never to rise (even as zombies.)

The Great Escape From Amazon's Walled Garden is Easy

Lots of successful authors do this every day.

And you don't even have to take your ebook out of KDP Select.

Amazon is asking for trouble by getting into print versions, but it's a logical extension of what they've been doing already. As they are also starting up independent bookstores, this is also going to increase their market share and get them scrutinized by the government, leading to their forced restructuring. They are making competition too difficult for other people to break free. (See Coker article again for how this is predicted to work out.)

But that is their problem, not ours.

The successful authors I've followed (Mark Dawson, Nick Stephenson, Joanna Penn, Steve Scott, among others) all started out with a slew of books up on Amazon as ebooks and finally had a breakthrough by promoting them on Facebook, stacking those ads with other promotion such as Bookbub and appearing on podcasts and other shows.

Here's what's really interesting:

- they then got all the *other versions* available,
- they built and started running *courses*,
- some also started getting *paid speaking gigs*,
- and they also got into *affiliate marketing* those courses,
- so they quit writing as many books (too busy.)
- And their income stayed up, but they were no longer as dependent on Amazon ebook sales.

Did you catch that? This actually follows those curves above. **Once these authors figured out how to leverage Amazon, then they got their own audiences and diversified their**

product lines. *Successful authors turned their writing into a business and started running that business.*

It's just too simple. <u>See my earlier post about the Author Platform</u>. They built their networks, their audience, and their content so that *they were no longer dependent solely on Amazon for their income*. They followed their vision and attained it.

Deep Backbench Plus Multiple Eyeballs Equals Financial Freedom

That's the formula for success.

1. Publish a lot of books people want in a series.
2. Get these available in all possible formats, on all possible marketplaces and sales outlets.
3. Run remunerative promotion that pays for itself. Get your content in front of all possible audiences that would appreciate it and buy it. Build an audience you can promote to effectively.
4. Encourage your audience to not just share it, but become evangelists and get cut in for a share of your income.

The formula for ebook author slavery: keep feeding the beast with new books in the hope that they will continue raising the sales of your other books. You have to publish every thirty days to be effective at this. (Or go the Patterson route where you think up thousands of plots and "co-author" or hire ghostwriters to crank out so much content you can distribute your own brand of consumable fiction.)

I've been saying this for years. *If you're going to be successful, then you have to model other's successes.* Build a brand and encourage your network and audience to share with their networks and audience. And reward them for it.

Too simple. More work than ebooks, but not too much if you organize it right.

What you face up to a bully and hit where it hurts, they run away and bother you no more. Once the word gets out, they bother no one any more. Amazon had a nice run in book selling. That's why they diversified into selling everything else and even making rockets and drones. They are overripe for disruption. It's now only a matter of time...

VI - Who's buying what?

Some notes here:

Amazon has around 70% of the ebook market, according to Author Earnings reports. Ebooks are about 30% of the market, which means Amazon ebooks are about 20% of the International book sales. So another 80% of sales they don't control in ebooks. Long tail stuff.

Another report has Amazon selling about 50% of the hardcopy books (which isn't substantiated, and mostly comes from the Big 5 which are known to be wrong more often than right with their statistics.)

In other places, I note that books are "idea containers" and that there are multiple versions of books. Audio books are gathering a larger percentage of sales.

Key point here is that people don't buy just one version of a book, this is Amazon's push for their audio sales along with the ebook. (They haven't figured out how to have a print book read aloud to you... yet.)

All this last essay covers is that there is no one story you have to understand to create (and test) a business plan. That plan you can use to maximize your income and also your satisfaction with the life you want to live.

Practically, you could sell nothing on Amazon and earn as much or more income elsewhere. One of those, for instance, would be creating and delivering courses. Amazon doesn't do courses – yet. Might not ever, as it's not their expertise. Of course, they could buy Udemy or one of the other marketplaces and then integrate it into their sales structure...

Right now, though, you can make tons of money on all the other market places besides Kindle ebooks. The Internet Marketer "guru's" want to sell you the Get Rich Quick route, which isn't working any more. But that is what the IM guys do – get in, make their fast bucks off the naïve, and move on.

That's why I wrote this particular essay – to clue you in to the alternatives.

VII - Don't Waste Your Book Publishing Time. Invest it.

Because you can get a return on money, and gain it all back if you lose everything. Lots of people do. Trump did, Napoleon Hill did, the list is a long one.

But the list of people who got their <u>time</u> back is exactly ZERO.

There is more than a lot of crap out there about how to succeed in book publishing and "make money" with Amazon. But get your waders out. It will only get worse the more you get into it.

I've signed up for a lot of Facebook Private Groups in the past few months. All with these people who say they are going to help me "get my book published." And so on, and so on. I've already been through their courses and found out that while they had a few good points, the majority was stuff you could pick up anywhere.

So I was busy over the holidays and most of January publishing books. Lots of books. And I've said before that Social Media is a big time suck.

But I was snookered sideways onto an FB group today, where they stashed their videos. And looked up in the corner to see some 33 entries there. I pulled that down and saw it was the typical crap Zuckerberg thinks people want – to see people in your "network" liking cat pictures and so on. I was expecting to see some group activity. But for about two months, there was only one of my groups that was active. One. Out of maybe a dozen or more. And that was the one with the cheapest and skinniest course I had paid for. There was lots of data, but he's mostly put it into that FB group, where you can download audio and so on. And he's got other courses on Udemy and I've got them all as MP3's so I can listen to them like podcasts whenever I want.

Get this, though: his course is the *least* expensive (under $100 with a discount coupon) and *the FB group is where he put the extra data*. The FB Group is the *actual* course. Yeah, weird, huh?

And that's the *only* active group. The *only* one. People actually contributing and getting real questions answered.

For all those $500, 800, 900-dollar courses? *Crickets.*

The only thing I've heard from those course-builders is Affiliate offers they want me to buy in on.

So what does this have to do with you?

Here's some datums to absorb:

Conventional Wisdom is 99% wrong. Look up quotes on that subject if you don't believe me. Will Rogers had some great ones.

The main problem is that our culture is set to invent and forward fake news as if is were fact. And it's not. Never has been. And that fake conventional wisdom is where the vast majority of all these book publishing courses sit.

This keeps going because every one of us has been carefully trained to do three things:

Not Look, Not Think, and Not Act.

Like when lots of someone's get most people repeating that "social media is where it's at." Then you really want to know who they are following and if someone up ahead really knows where they are actually going.

Because *social media doesn't get you real friends* and doesn't make your family life better. But old Zuckerburg has all your private data in his system so that you get the ads in that sidebar that you can't shut off and they are every bit as insulting and condescending as they are on TV. You don't need that stuff. Any of it.

You've got to shake off those shackles you've been trained to wear.

- You have to observe for yourself.
- You have to think things through, test everything you're hearing or reading or viewing.
- And you've got to act when you know it's the right thing to do. Not hesitate, not "sleep on it."

Book publishing is dead simple. Book marketing is a *lot* simpler than you've been told.

Every time I figure something out, I test it over and over. Then when I know it works for me, and will probably work for you, I tell you.

Maybe I blog it. Often, I'll write it up in a book. Sometimes, it winds up in a podcast. A few PDF's, a few videos.

But I don't sit on anything. Because of that Golden Rule. You have to give before you can get, and you can only get as good as you give.

If you've got questions, I've got an email you can find. Someone from the Netherlands emailed me the other day about a book I'd published several years ago. I thanked him and asked him if he needed anything else, and then sent him another PDF of a related book that might help him.

And occasionally I find some real people who actually answer their emails. These people are gold. Treat them right and let them know how valuable they are.

Take these tips today:

- Look over the time you spend on social media and see if you couldn't do something better with it. But social media doesn't sell books. Never has.

- Look over what you are spending your time on and see if it's a good use, a good return on your investment.

Bonus

Who Else Wants to Write Bestsellers That Become Classics?

Get No-Charge Access to Writing and Publishing Materials from Our Library Collection

Instant Access - Join Here

Click or type into your browser:

http://livesensical.com/go/writingbooks/